The Circle Time

Handbook

The Circle Time

Handbook

39 Best Ever
Group Activities
For Toddler to Teens

Lora Langston

Copyright 2016

To those who work in the trenches everyday,
not just to make a living but to make a difference.

Contents

Circle Time Games, Activities, & Ideas
Why do Circle Time?
Dance Freeze
Bug in a Rug
Pass the Movement
Shake the Sillies Out
Circle Time Collaborative Painting
Click, Clack, Moo Story Starter
Animal Movement Game
Quiet as a Mouse
Calendar Time
Alphabet Store
Talking Stick
Day of the Week Bags
Pass the Facial Expression
Play Duck, Duck, Goose
Drip Drip Splash
Nature Based Circle Activity
Easter Egg Pass Game
Bunny Train Game
Lucky's Coins
Jump to the End of the Rainbow
Little Leprechaun Corners
The Crazy Question Game
Players sit in a circle and pass out paper. Ask the players to write a question on one side of the paper but don't let them answer it.
This is a What?
Windows and Doors
Village Chief
Stick Numbers or Alien Language
Splat
Buzz
Bob The Weasel
Dead Horse
Crocodile Morey
Honey if You Love Me…
The group starts in a circle with one person in the middle.
Grandma's Underpants
Escape From the Monsters
Ha Ha Ha!
Zoomy Zoomy
Monster, Aliens, Wizards
Important Stuff

Circle Time Games, Activities, & Ideas

Circle Time is an important part of every preschool program, but circle activities work for older children too. Group time, gathering time, whatever you name it, the act of gathering around in a circle is a wonderful way to start and end the day. With all eyes on the leader, it builds a sense of togetherness making the perfect time for bonding.

Preschool Circle Time is for Group Lessons, Games, and Interaction. These ideas help build a sense of community, a time for sharing, and a fun learning environment for little ones.

For older students, circle time or group gathering time, is often used as a way to introduce students to each other. Sitting staring into a sea of unknown faces is intimidating. To help kids get to know each other, group leaders should plan simple icebreaker activities.

Circle Time is also a way to transition to new activities in camp programs. It is a meeting of minds, a time and place to share knowledge, to give instruction, to enjoy fellowship, and to teach new things.

Running out of ideas for Preschool Circle Time? Every preschool program needs circle time for group interaction. This is a time to build structure into the program. Let the children know what to expect each day. It is valuable to offer circle time at least twice a day. Once in the morning and once just before time to go home.

We've compiled several ideas for group time activities for your program.

Sometimes, it is difficult to remember all of the steps for each activity. Thumbing through a book in front of the children takes valuable time away from more pertinent activities. Each activity is on it's own page, so that you can make a copy for your clipboard.

Print a copy of each activity. Share it with your staff, and send it home with parents.

Songs for Camp or After School Programs:
http://www.kidscreativechaos.com/2015/07/circle-activities-for-teens-middle.htm

Why do Circle Time?

Circle Time plays an important role in childhood development. A successful circle time is interactive, educational, and fun!

If you hated Circle Time as a child, ask yourself why? Likely, your instructor was doing it wrong. Maybe you felt left out or singled out?

Did you sit in a circle forced to sit still? Were you forced to sit quietly with eyes directed at the teacher at all times. That's no fun! It isn't educational either. The only valuable take away from those type of experiences is that children are to be seen and not heard. Sitting perfectly still is stressful to some children. They learn to dread what is possibly the most important part of any child centered program.

Circle Time builds a sense of community. It grows friendship bonds and lasting memories. We all have memories of our time in the circle. Let's make sure future generations have joyful ones.

When you implement these activities, add visual elements, tactile objects, fun sounds, and even scents. Adding sensory elements to your group gatherings not only insures a memorable experience but also heightens the learning experience.

Sensory Play isn't just for babies and toddlers. Teens and adults are more likely to engage and remember when the senses are involved.

Including sensory elements is Circle Time activities gets the creative juices flowing. Bored with the same old games? Ask your group to brainstorm new elements, chants, or movements to the old favorites. They will appreciate being included in the conversation, and you will discover new ways to interact with your group.

Why do Circle Time? Because, a sense of community and socialization can validate self-worth.

Dance Freeze

Large open space. Indoors or outdoors. All ages.

Dance freeze is one of those ideas that makes you feel like you were the first to invent it when your were a kid. It is so simple, but oh so magical. Kids want to play it again and again.

Explain the rules to this game while sitting in the circle. Then, have everyone stand up within the circle to play. As each person gets out, sit them in the center of the circle so they don't get squished by the other dancers. With larger groups, spread out across a field or in a gym.

Play some music on your phone, tablet, or a good, old-fashioned radio. If you are musically inclined, sing a tune!

Explain to the group that as long as the song is playing, they can dance willy nilly. When the music stops, they must freeze in their dancing position- one leg in the air, hands on hip, whatever they were doing last.

Abruptly stop the song; don't sing or wait until the end of a verse, that is too predictable.

No moving, blinking, or twitching allowed. If they move, they must sit frozen in that spot, criss-cross applesauce, and wait to see who stays frozen the longest.

Once officially out, move the sitters to the center of the circle.

The first ones out will happily help patrol the other players for illegal movement.

Bug in a Rug

Large open space. Indoors or outdoors. Toddlers to kindergarteners.

Sit everyone in a circle. Grab a blanket or a big beach towel. Pick one child to leave the room or to <u>wear a fun blindfold</u>.

Teacher picks a student.

Shh! Just point at the child, grab their hand, and take them away from the group. Now, point at another child and then to the 'rug.'

Hide the child under the 'rug.'

Bring the other person back.

Can they guess who is missing?

Pass the Movement

Large open space. Indoors or outdoors. All ages.

Leader starts with a movement.

Perhaps, you wave your hand in the air.

Now, the person sitting to your right must wave their hand and add a movement like wiggling their nose.

The next person to the right does those movements and adds one of their own.

Play continues until every person has had a chance to add a movement of their own.

This becomes a 'WAVE' of different movements.

Add sensory elements by placing musical instruments, squishy toys, or other objects in the center of the circle to use with the movements.

Players can choose an item or simply make up a move.

Shake the Sillies Out

Large open space. Indoors or outdoors. All ages. Ideal for preschoolers.

Need a game to get kids' moving? Find some *Dragon Tunes* from the cartoon, *Dragon Tales*, and every morning, "Shake the Sillies Out!"

Just play the song, and follow the instructions. Kids love this one!

If you don't have, *Dragon Tunes,* any fun song will do.

Circle Time Collaborative Painting

Large open space. Indoors or outdoors. All ages. Great for Team Building.

Leader lays out a big roll of paper and painting supplies. Everyone paints concentric circles. Pass the painting, and make a PROGRESSIVE PAINTING. This idea teaches patience. Everyone must wait their turn.

Lay out a large painting tarp, sit the children in a circle on the tarp, give each child a cup of paint and a brush. Give out as many colors as possible, but only one color per person. No painting unless it is your turn.

To make it less frustrating, pass two large poster boards around the circle starting at opposite ends. Children are allowed to paint only one circle or shape of their choice per turn.

While they are painting, share an art lesson on shapes, talk about teamwork, or sing a fun song!

Click, Clack, Moo Story Starter

Large open space. Indoors or outdoors. Preschool to Sixth grade.

You know the story about the unhappy cows in the barn? They have a typewriter. They make demands. An electric blanket would be nice.

What else might the <u>farm animals</u> want from the farmer?

Play <u>a Circle Time Game</u> where each child is given an animal. Before the game, print out cards with farm animal pictures on one side and the name of the animal on the other side.

Each child draws a card from a hat.

Give this example to the kids: What does the (insert animal here) pig want? "Dear Farmer Brown, the barn is smelly. Please send air fresheners."

Have each child come up with their own idea for what the animal on the card might want from the farmer.

Choose different stories to change the game. Try, *The Cat in the Hat* or *Harry Potter*, with older children.

Animal Movement Game

Large open space. Indoors or outdoors. Preschoolers to Third grade.

Take the Story Starter game one step further.

Get the kids moving like the animals.

Ask, "What does a pig say?"

"How does a pig move?"

The children take turns walking around the circle pretending they are the animal on their card.

Quiet as a Mouse

Large open space. Indoors or outdoors. Preschoolers.

When Circle Time is done, keep children in a circle to release them to the next activity.

Leader: "The child who sits as quiet as a mouse gets to line up next."

Continue until everyone or almost everyone (we don't like to single out those who can't sit still or quiet) is in line.

Calendar Time

Large open space. Indoors or outdoors. Preschool to First grade.

Sing: "Sunday, Monday, Tuesday Wednesday, Thursday Friday, Saturday. Suunday, Munday... TUUESday."

Emphasize the current day of the week.

Sing the song and then check the calendar.

Ask: "Who can find today on the calendar?"

Alphabet Store

Large open space. Indoors or outdoors. Preschool to Sixth grade.

Using the first letter of each child's name, pretend to go shopping for an item that begins with that letter.

For example, "Jake will buy a jump rope."

With older kids, have everyone repeat each person's item. If one player forgets something, the entire group must start over. Those who have already had a turn must stick with their original purchase.

Continue around the circle until everyone has had a turn.

This game helps with letter recognition and memorization.

Talking Stick

Any open space will do. Indoors or outdoors. All ages.

Bring in a cane or recycle a cardboard wrapping paper tube.

During Circle Time, grab the stick.

Explain that this is a talking stick. Only the person who holds it may speak. Pass it around the circle taking turns to share or introduce yourself.

This is a great tool to use for *Show and Tell* or other situations where children take turns sharing.

Companion Activity: Have the kids make their own 'Talking Stick' with Washi or Duct Tape, Glitter, or Feathers.

Day of the Week Bags

Any open space will do. Indoors or outdoors. Preschool to Kindergarten.

Make a brown paper bag for each day of the week.

Prep a calendar on Poster Board.

Give each bag a colorful label.

Fill the bag with the names of classmates who have birthdays on this day or other special things that happen on this day of THIS week.

Hand the bags around the circle at random intervals.

Play some music or sing a song.

When the music stops, the person holding the bag opens it.

Leader gives each person with the bag a sticker.

They must place their sticker on the proper day of the week.

This is a nice companion activity to the *Day of the Week* song.

Pass the Facial Expression

Any space will do. All ages.

Hold up magazine pictures of facial expressions.

Ask: "What is this person feeling?"

Have the children take turns making the face in the picture.

Then, pass the facial expression. Game plays like the game *Telephone*.

After you play this game, give each child a mirror.

Have them draw a selfie with their favorite expression.

Companion Activity: Emotion Art Lesson.
http://www.kidscreativechaos.com/2012/09/art-elementary-home-school-projects.html

Play Duck, Duck, Goose

Large open space. Indoors or outdoors. All ages.

This old standby might seem boring, but it is likely new to the toddlers and preschoolers in your class. Change it up each day. With a few tweaks, it is fun for all ages!

After they get the hang of the game, add a creative play element by acting it out. Have the kids act and walk like the animal as they toddle around.

For older or school-age children, change the theme to *Pig, Pig, Cow* or *Ghost, Ghost, Vampire* or *Bunny, Bunny, Chick* (must hop around the circle). The more creative, the better.

Participants sit down in a circle facing each other. One person is 'it' and walks around the outside of the circle gently tapping the other players on the head and saying either 'duck' or 'goose'.

When a person is tapped on the head and called 'goose', they stand up and chase the person who is 'it' around the outside of the circle trying to tag 'it' before that player can sit down in the spot where the 'goose' was sitting.

If the 'goose' is able to tag 'it', then the 'goose' can return back to his seat.

'It' repeats the same procedure again. If 'it' sits before being tagged by the 'goose,' then the 'goose' becomes 'it' and the game starts again.

See a fun variation for summer camp on the next page.

Drip Drip Splash

Any open space will do. Indoors or outdoors. All ages.

Supplies: Cup of water, hot summer day

Similar to *Duck Duck Goose*.

Instead of touching the heads of those not picked, sprinkle a bit of water on each of their heads as you walk around the circle.

The 'Goose' gets all of the leftover water poured on their head.

Snowball Scoop

Large open space. Indoors or outdoors. All ages.

Supplies: One or two bags of cotton balls, bowls, spoons, blindfold

Players form a circle.

Blindfold the first players. Sit three to five players in the middle of the circle to scoop up as many cotton balls as they can within thirty seconds using only their spoon. No hands!

The middle of the circle is filled with snowballs (cotton balls).

Once the players are seated, give them bowls and spoons.

Jingle a bell to signify the start of the game.

The player with the most snowballs in the bowl wins.

Nature Based Circle Activity

Large open space. Indoors or outdoors. All ages, particularly preschoolers.

Perception changes when senses are limited. Didi of *Duck, Duck, Octopus* shared this game with us on Kidscreativechaos.com.

Gather natural objects (e.g. a dandelion, rock, shell, lobster claw, stick, cattail fluff, maple leaf, an animal bone, feather, dirt, etc.). Collect one item per child. Keep collection stored out of sight.

Place one mystery object in a brown lunch bag. Fold the flap over and seal. Place the bags in a box or 'treasure chest'.

Talk about the diversity of nature: Have the kids offer examples of colors, textures, and shapes they may find in nature.

Using the kids' examples, make connections to how we use senses to experience the world.

Explain that each mystery bag contains one object found in nature. They must try to guess what is in their bag without using their sense of sight, sound, or taste.

Each child chooses a mystery bag and keeps it tightly closed.

Children should fully explore their object with their sense of touch and smell. If they go to smell the bag, they have to keep their eyes shut or use a blindfold to help keep the mystery object hidden. The child exploring the item tells the group about the object based on their sensory observations.

> For example, if the object is a dandelion, a child may describe it as follows: There is a fluffy, soft part on one end. It is round. The round, soft part is stuck to something that is long and skinny. It smells like grass.

Ask the child doing the sensory exploration to identify their mystery object. Then, open the inquiry to the group. Does anyone think the object is something else?

Reveal the mystery object.

When the object is revealed most of the kids will know what it is right away. If they don't guess correctly, ask the kids how their sense of sight, sound, or taste would have helped them to solve the mystery.

Easter Egg Pass Game

Large open space. Indoors or outdoors. All ages.

Supplies: Plastic Eggs, Large Spoons, Easter Basket

Object: Pass the ball back and forth without dropping it.

Give each player a large ladle or spoon.

Each group of two players needs a **plastic Easter egg**.

Player one starts with the egg balanced on his spoon. He tosses it to his teammate who tries to catch the egg in his spoon.

With a larger group of children, at a **kid's birthday party**, play a variation of this game by dividing the group in half and lining everyone up into a single file line. Ask them to pass the egg down.

When you say, "On your mark, get set, go", the race begins. The egg is passed from spoon to spoon until it gets to the person at the end of the line. If the egg is dropped, the team must start over.

The last person in line drops the egg into an Easter basket at the end of the line to win.

Variation: The fastest team wins! As an alternative, give each team an equal number of eggs and a time limit. When you blow the whistle, everyone must freeze. The team with the most eggs in their Easter basket wins.

Bunny Train Game

Any open space will do. Indoors or outdoors. Toddlers to Tweens.

Supplies: Plastic Eggs, Easter Basket, 1 Easter Bonnet, bunny ears for all players

Before the game begins, use a permanent marker to mark one of the plastic eggs with bunny ears.

Everyone sits in a circle wearing bunny ears. Place the basket of eggs and the bonnet in the center of the circle. Choose one player to hop around the circle like a bunny.

The bunny chooses another player by tapping him on the shoulder.

The second player places his hands on the first player's shoulders (like a train). They continue to hop around the circle adding new players to their bunny train.

The last player stays seated and then grabs the basket and the bonnet.

The bunny train circles him and then sits down. The player with the basket passes one egg to each of the other players. The player who gets the bunny egg must trade his ears for the bonnet.

Eggs are placed back into the basket. Everyone wearing bunny ears forms a new circle around the basket of eggs. The player in the Easter bonnet is now 'it'. Play continues until everyone has a chance to be 'it.'

For a more festive game, play the songs *Bunny Hop* and *Easter Bonnet*.

Companion Activity: Make your own ears and bonnets.

Lucky's Coins

Any open space will do. Indoors or outdoors. Toddlers to Tweens.

Object: Follow the coin trail, collect the coins, and find Lucky's hiding spot.
Leader: "Did you know if you catch a Leprechaun he has to grant you three wishes?"

Give little pots of gold or mini Leprechaun hats to each player.

Hide the coins all around the play area.

Send kids on a hunt for the gold treasure.

The player who finds the most coins wins.

Hide leprechauns at the end of the rainbow (coin trail).

The one who finds the leprechaun gets to keep it.

Companion Activity: Make pots of gold and little leprechaun hats from cardboard tubes. You can make gold coins or buy them. Find a hat tutorial here:
http://www.kidscreativechaos.com/2013/05/cardboard-tube-crafts-hey-its-toilet.html

Jump to the End of the Rainbow

Any open space will do. Indoors or outdoors. Toddlers to Tweens.

Supplies: Find an area inside or outside where you can mark six to eight feet in a straight line. Add a SENSORY PLAY element by using a roll of bubble wrap. Glitter serves as magic dust.

Prep: With a permanent marker, write the name of the player(s) on a fake gold coin. To add an ART element to the game have the kids make their own coins with cardboard and construction paper. Coins are used to mark landing spots.

Leader: "Leprechauns use magic to boost their jumps. Let me sprinkle some magic dust over you."

Each player stands at one end of the bubble wrap or marked area. Make a start and finish line with jump rope or masking tape.

With both feet together, the player swings his arms back and jumps forward as far as he can.

Place a coin on the spot where the back of the jumper's heel lands.

MATH ELEMENT: Have players measure the distance from the start line to the coin. How far did they jump?

Give everyone several turns to see if they can out jump their previous score.

Little Leprechaun Corners

Any open space will do. Indoors or outdoors. Toddlers to Teens.

Supplies: Carpet squares, construction paper in rainbow colors, a Leprechaun hat, and music

Place a different color in four corners of your space. Carpet sample squares work for the four corners, but construction paper works too.

To help students learn about Irish culture, find Bagpipe music or Irish ballads.

Leader: "When the music plays, move around anyway you want. This is the perfect time to go crazy and shake the sillies out! When the music stops, choose a corner and run to it."

When all players have chosen a corner, pull a color from the rainbow out of a Leprechaun's hat. Everyone in that corner is out and must sit down.

Start the music again. Repeat until there is one child left in a corner.

The winner wears the Leprechaun hat for the day.

The Crazy Question Game

Any open space will do. Indoors or outdoors. All ages.

Players sit in a circle and pass out paper. Ask the players to write a question on one side of the paper but don't let them answer it.

Collect the papers. Give them back at random, making sure that nobody has the question that they wrote.

Tell them to write the answer to the question on the back. It can be as silly or crazy as they want.

Collect the papers again.

Pass them back out randomly.

The first player starts and reads the question to the person beside them.

The person beside them reads the answer on their own paper.

Play continues clockwise.

This is a What?

Any open space will do. Indoors or outdoors. All ages.

Group sits in a circle. You'll need several objects which you pass from hand to hand around the circle (doll, cap, toy car, etc.).

The leader starts by looking to the person next to him and holding up the object in his hand.

He says, "this is a doll."

She responds, "a what?"

He says, "a doll."

She says, "a what?"

He says, "a shoe."

She takes the doll and says, "oh, a doll!"

She then turns to the next person and starts the same interaction with that person.

The leader adds more items. They all start at the same and join into the same rhythm.

The goal is to have as many items going around as there are people in the circle.

Players turns to the player on one side and say what the item is and then says, "a what" to the player on the other side.

Goal: See how fast items can pass around the circle.

Windows and Doors

Any open space will do. Indoors or outdoors. Toddlers to Teens.

Kids form a circle holding hands. They spread out enough so that everyone's arms are straightened out forming large spaces between them.

These are the windows and doors.

One child runs and weaves in and out between the other children. As they do this, the kids in the circle randomly drop their arms down trying to touch or trap the person who is weaving in and out.

Once the person is caught or touched by the arms of someone else, they are out.

The person outed gets to choose which person is next to weave in and out of the windows and doors.

Village Chief

Any open space will do. Indoors or outdoors. Toddlers to Tweens.

Everyone sits in a circle.

One person leaves.

Another person is selected as the 'Village Chief' or the 'It.'

Everyone else in the circle has to follow the movements of the 'Chief' (clapping, snapping, banging the ground).

The person who stepped out of the circle comes back and tries to see whose movements everyone else is following.

They must guess who is the 'Chief.'

Stick Numbers or Alien Language

Any open space will do. Indoors or outdoors. Toddlers to Tweens.

One leader has several sticks.

The leader makes up a random combination with the sticks and says, "This is a secret language; the sticks spell out a number one to ten and one to ten only."

Make as many stick figures and arrangements as you want, it doesn't matter, as long as you are making numbers with your hands.

Say it is a five, all you have to do is put your hand on the ground and spread out your fingers.

The fingers that you make numbers with must be on the ground and visible at all times.

Players are looking at the sticks.

If players can't get it, tell a few the secret and have them guess the answer.

Splat

Any open space will do. Indoors or outdoors. All ages.

Everyone stands in a circle, one person is nominated as the splatterer.

The Splatterer stands in the middle. The person in the middle randomly points at someone else and shouts, "Splat!"

The person they pointed at must duck. The two people on either side of the one who ducked must "splat" each other, by pointing at each other and yelling, "Splat!"

The last one to do this is out.

This continues until there are only two active people left in the circle.

Once out, they must stay in the circle, but they do not continue to play. This is part of the challenge for the remaining players.

With less players in action, it becomes harder to determine who is next as the numbers diminish and the circle size remains.

Once down to the last two active players in the circle, they stand back to back like in an old west showdown.

The person who was in the middle counts from one to twenty.

With each number, the two remaining players must take a step away from one another.

At any random point between one and twenty, the counter shouts 'splat' instead of a number.

Then, they take a quick draw on each other.

The last one to point at their opponent and say 'splat' is out.

Buzz

Any open space will do. Indoors or outdoors. All ages.

'It' (the leader) picks a secret number.

The first person starts by saying 'one'.

Starting to that person's left, each person will say either the next sequential number, or the word 'Buzz'.

When they reach the leader's number (the goal number), play stops.

When someone says 'Buzz' the direction of play reverses. Play may start clockwise and end up counter clockwise.

If someone in the group makes a mistake, the group starts the process over with the person who made the mistake re-starting the round.

Buzz Rules:
The following numbers are to be replaced with the word 'Buzz'.
Any number that is a multiple of three (3,6,9,12,15…)
Any number that is a multiple of seven (7,14,21,28…)
Any number with double digits (11,22,33…)

Example:
One, two, buzz (reverse direction), four, five, six, buzz (reverse direction), eight, buzz (reverse direction), ten, buzz (reverse direction), buzz (reverse direction), thirteen, Buzz (reverse direction), and so on…

Bob The Weasel

Any open space will do. Indoors or outdoors. All ages.

One person steps into the center of the circle.

The outside group puts their arms around each other as if in a huddle.

Next, they pass an object around the outside of the circle.

While turning slowly, the person on the inside of the circle must try to guess who has the object.

The group jumps up and down shouting, "Bob the Weasel, keep it goin' keep it going."

If the person inside the circle has their back turned to the person in the circle holding 'Bob', that circle member holds up the object and then everyone shouts, "I saw the weasel, I saw the weasel."

Continue chanting, "Bob the Weasel, Keep it Goin' keep it Going.'"

When the player in the middle guesses who has the weasel, the player holding the weasel goes into the middle.

Dead Horse

Any open space will do. Indoors or outdoors. Toddlers to Tweens.

Somebody lies down and closes their eyes while everyone else gathers around them.

The one lying down must keep their eyes closed while the others try to make him laugh without touching him.

When the person lying down laughs, he loses.

Now, another person lies down to play the dead horse.

Crocodile Morey

Any open space will do. Indoors or outdoors. Toddlers to Tweens.

Everyone sits in a circle with hands out to their sides and palms up.

Everyone's right hand is on top of their neighbors left (palms up).

The leader starts the song. When the song starts, the first person takes their right hand, crosses it over to the person on their left and *gently* slaps that person's right hand. This continues until the end of the song.

On the last word of the song, two things can happen. First, when the group sings out, "Five," the person whose hand is slapped is out. Second, if this person is quick enough and pulls their hand away in time before the other person slaps their hand, then the person trying to slap is out.

The circle moves in closer and continues playing.

When down to two people, they stand up, hold each other's right hand in front of them and sing the song again while swinging their joined hands back and forth toward each other in rhythm to the song.

When they say, "Five," the person that their hands are closer to is out. The other player is the winner.

Crocodile morey, croc, croc, croc.

See cinco, cinco, - cinco, cinco sock.

See cinco, cinco, - malo, malo, - malo, malo, malo.

One, two, three, four, five!

Honey if You Love Me...

Any open space will do. Indoors or outdoors. Toddlers to Teens.

The group starts in a circle with one person in the middle.

This person in the middle tries to get others to laugh by saying, "Honey if you love me, you'll smile."

The person on the outside must respond without smiling or laughing saying, "Honey, I love you, but I just can't smile."

The person in the middle does various things without touching anyone to get the other person to smile.

If the person in the middle does make another player smile, that player moves to the center of the circle.

Grandma's Underpants

Any open space will do. Indoors or outdoors. All ages.

The group sits in a circle.

One person is 'it.'

'It' stands in the middle of the circle.

The kids on the outside of the circle ask the 'it' questions.

The only thing the 'it' can say is, "My grandma's under pants."

The object is to try to make 'it' laugh.

Once someone makes 'it' laugh, they become 'it.'

Escape From the Monsters

Any open space will do. Indoors or outdoors. Kindergarteners to Teens.

Four monsters are chosen, blindfolded, and placed in the middle of a circle.

These Monsters sit on their treasure.

Balls or bean bags are used as ammunition.

The leader chooses one brave person to go through the circle and steal the treasure.

This person gets three monster deactivators (crepe paper tied into a circle). This will de-activate the monsters when held over their heads.

The monsters can stop trespassers by hitting them with a ball or bean bag.

The players in the circle help the monsters by telling them where to find the trespasser.

Ha Ha Ha!

Any open space will do. Indoors or outdoors. All ages.

Everyone lies in a circle with each other's heads on each other's stomachs.

On 'go,' the first person will shout 'Ha,' and then it is repeated one by one clockwise around the circle.

Everyone's heads bounce up on the other person's stomach when 'Ha' is shouted.

The next player, shouts two 'Ha Ha's,' and it goes around again.

The next player, shouts three 'Ha Ha's,' and so on...

Continue doing this until everyone has had a turn shouting 'Ha.'

Zoomy Zoomy

Any open space will do. Indoors or outdoors. All ages.

Children sit in a circle. The leader is 'Zoomy Zoomy.'

Everybody else is a number one, two, three, and so on...

Clap your lap twice and snap twice to make a pattern.

Zoomy Starts by chanting, "Zoomy Zoomy, Zoomy ZooMa, Zoomy Zoomy, Zoomy ZooMa" to the pattern.

Zoomy calls out a number twice. The player with the corresponding number has to repeat the number and say another number. Someone else says 'Zoomy.'

The first one to make a mistake is out.

Those who are out sit it the middle of the circle.

Game play continues.

"Zoomy Zoomy, Zoomy ZooMa, Zoomy Zoomy, Zoomy ZooMa."

Zoomy Zoomy (the leader) says,"Zoomy Zoomy, seven, seven."

Player with the number seven says, "seven, seven, two, two."

Player with the number two says, "two, two, Zoomy Zoomy."

Zoomy Zoomy says, "Zoomy Zoomy, three, three."

The player with the number three says, "five, five."

This is wrong, they didn't say their number at the beginning. Number three is out.

The game continues until only one number remains in play.

Monster, Aliens, Wizards

Any open space will do. Indoors or outdoors. Preschoolers to Teens.

Monsters: Beat Elves. Action: Show that you are a monster by raising your arms high over your head and 'roaring' at the opposing team.

Wizards: Beat Monsters. Action: Show that you are wizard by pretending to shoot magic from your finger tips at the opposing team while making a loud 'zapping' sound.

Elves: Beat Wizards. Action: Show that you are an elf by sticking out your tongue and wiggling your fingers by your ears (as if mocking the other team). Make silly sounds.

Split the players into two even teams and designate one additional person as the referee.

Choose a place to play.

Mark a start, centerline, and a boundary line at the end of each side.

Each team huddles together at their own boundary line and decides which character they will be (as a team) at the beginning of each round.

Once the teams have decided, the ref calls them to the centerline and calls out, "One, two, three, go!"

The teams do the action for the character they chose. If their character beats the opposing team's character, they will chase them back to their boundary line tagging as many players as they can and bringing those players to their team.

Play continues until one team captures all of the players from the other team.

This is similar to the game, *Rock Paper Scissors*.

Important Stuff

Once you've completed all of these games, visit our website for more games and activities: kidscreativechaos.com This book is also available on eReaders; check it out for clickable links.

Do you have a group game? We would love to hear about it. If we like your idea, we'll publish it on our website.

These games are in the public domain. We've been playing most of them since the late Eighties. The rest were taught to us during camps and afterschool programs. Please let us know if you play a different variation.

Did you find a mistake? We're human. Humans make mistakes. Send us a note. We'll make the correction, and send you a tweet.

info@theplayconnection.com

Printed in Great Britain
by Amazon